DK Publishing

TO THE EXTREME

A SLACKLINER BALANCES HIS WAY TOWARD LOST ARROW SPIRE, YOSEMITE NATIONAL PARK.

LONDON, NEW YORK, MUNICH, MELBOURNE, and DELHI

Written and edited by Penny Smith
Designed by Mary Sandberg, Karen Hood
Additional research, writing, and editing Lee Wilson, Wendy Horobin, Caroline Stamps, Fleur Star
Additional design Sadie Thomas, Pamela Shiels, Gemma Fletcher
US editor Margaret Parrish
Production editor Sean Daly
Jacket editor Matilda Gollon
Publishing manager Bridget Giles
Art director Martin Wilson
Creative director Jane Bull
Category publisher Mary Ling

First published in the United States in 2011 by
DK Publishing
375 Hudson Street
New York, New York 10014

10 9 8 7 6 5 4 3 2 1
001–179465–July/11

Copyright © 2011 Dorling Kindersley Limited

A catalog record for this book is available from the Library of Congress.

ISBN: 978-0-7566-8233-0

Printed and bound by Hung Hing, China

Discover more at
www.dk.com

CONTENTS

4–9 SCARY SKYDIVING

10–13 FIGHTING FOREST FIRES

14–17 HIGH-ROPE WALKING

18–23 BUILDING UP INTO THE SKY

24–25 FISHING IN STORMY SEAS

26–29 CLEARING DEADLY LANDMINES

30–35 EXPLORING HIDDEN CAVES

36–39 COLLECTING SNAKE VENOM

40–41 TRUCKING ON SNOW AND ICE

42–47 CLIMBING UP ROCK FACES

48–51 WORKING UNDERWATER

52–53 SKIING DOWN STEEP MOUNTAINS

INTRO...

ENTER THIS BOOK and meet those who choose to walk on thin ropes across mountain chasms or head off to work in stormy seas. Watch a skier head down an impossibly steep mountain face or join a construction worker on a building so high that a harness is vital. *To the Extreme* features these (and many more) fearless people—so hold tight, and step into a world of high excitement and constant challenge.

54–57 MINING DEEP UNDERGROUND

58–63 TRAVELING IN OUTER SPACE

64–67 SURFING BIG WAVES

68–71 HELICOPTER TO THE RESCUE!

72–79 JUST PLAIN CRAZY

80–81 WHERE TO FIND THINGS AND ACKNOWLEDGMENTS

A SLIPPERY CLIMB IN AN ICE CAVE

YOU'RE SITTING IN A PLANE 13,000 ft (4,000 m) above ground. The door opens. You take a deep breath and leap... There's 60 long seconds of free-falling—time to perform acrobatics or join up with another skydiver—before you open your parachute for a safe landing.

THE MAXIMUM HEIGHT YOU CAN JUMP FROM WITHOUT OXYGEN IS 16,000 FT (4,900 M).

SKYDIVERS' DIARY

1 **Packing** It's important to make sure the parachute is packed properly so it opens safely. All equipment is checked twice.

2 **Liftoff** Skydivers board the plane—or hot air balloon or helicopter—and fly to the right height over the "drop zone."

3 **Time to jump** The door in the back of the plane opens and one or two at a time, the skydivers leap out...

THE FIRST PARACHUTE WAS DESIGNED BY THE ITALIAN ARTIST AND INVENTOR...

HOW FAST DO YOU FALL?

Average speed for free-falling.

Slow to this speed before opening a parachute.

Free-fall speed reached with practice.

Fastest recorded free-fall speed.

Average speed for a safe landing.

120
160–180
110
190
260–290
180
20 520
13
13
321
km/h
mph

Lines attach the canopy to the container on the skydiver's back.

The **canopy** (or parachute) catches the air and slows the skydiver down.

Pull on the **toggles** to steer.

To open his parachute
the skydiver throws a small pilot parachute into the air. This catches the wind and pulls out the main canopy. The skydiver always carries a reserve parachute in case the main one fails to open.

canopy

4 **Free fall** The first few seconds are scary: falling at speed with no parachute. But there's time for a few midair acrobatics…

5 **Deployment** At 2,500 ft (760 m) above ground the pilot chute is released, which pulls the main canopy from the container.

6 **Landing** It's vital to slow down and bend the knees for a gentle landing. Keep a look out for hazards, such as trees and lakes!

… LEONARDO DA VINCI, IN 1483. IT WASN'T TESTED UNTIL 500 YEARS LATER—BUT IT WORKED!

You don't need a parachute in a wind tunnel—but it feels exactly the same as a real free fall.

Tandem Many people make their first skydive as a tandem jump—strapped to a qualified skydiver. It takes only around 20 minutes of training to learn how to put on a harness, how to position your body in free fall, and how to land. Then you're ready to jump!

It's windy in here!
If you're too young or too nervous to skydive, you can get the same effect inside a vertical wind tunnel. The good news is, there's a safety net!

Static line Nervous beginners can start with a static line jump. For this the canopy is fastened to a strong rope inside of the plane. This pulls the canopy open when you jump. You do at least six hours of classroom training for a static line jump, learning about the equipment, how to control a canopy, and how to land safely.

Accelerated free fall
This is for the more adventurous novice skydiver. After classroom training, you jump with two instructors and have a minute of free fall on your very first jump! The instructors help you perform acrobatic tricks before you open your canopy and land in the drop zone.

FORMATIONS
Experienced skydivers often perform in groups to create brief but spectacular displays, such as this diamond shape. The world record for a free-fall formation is 400 people, who held a spiral shape for more than four seconds in 2008.

FUN IN FREE FALL

If you thought skydiving couldn't get any crazier, you could always try one of these...

THERE ARE 100 SKYDIVERS IN THIS!

Skyaking This bizarre form of skydiving involves free falling while sitting in a small canoe.

Sky surfing Solo skydivers perform jumps and turns in the air while strapped to a board. They ride the air like a surfer rides waves—but without the water.

Wingsuits Skydivers wear suits with extra flaps of material that catch the air between their outstretched arms and legs, slowing them down. They open their canopy before they land.

THE ONLY WAY IS DOWN

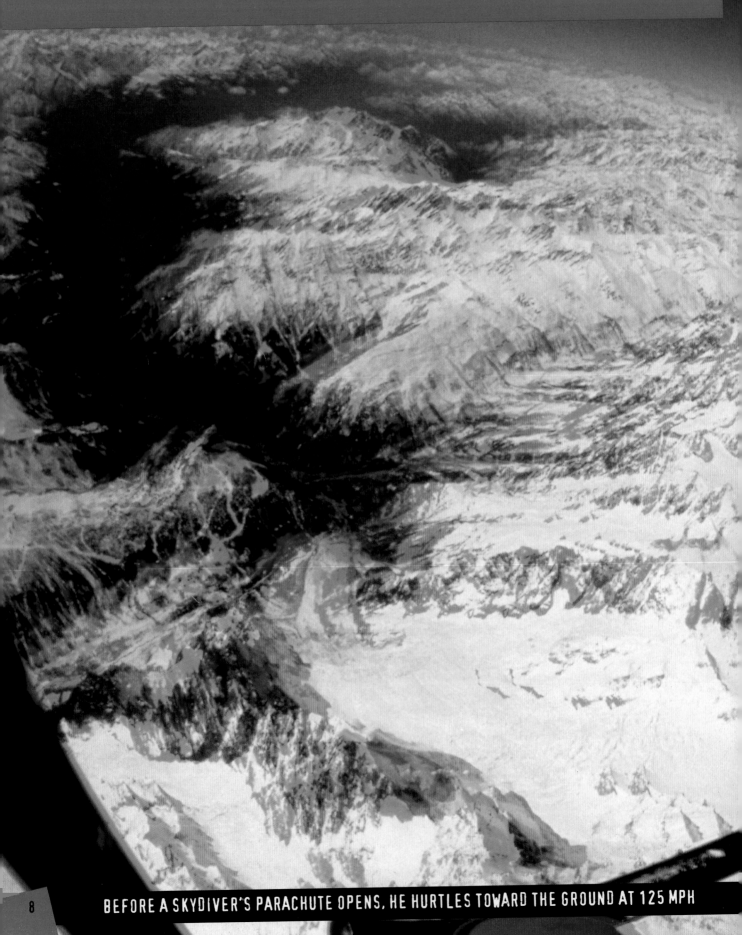

BEFORE A SKYDIVER'S PARACHUTE OPENS, HE HURTLES TOWARD THE GROUND AT 125 MPH

(200 KM/H). AMAZINGLY, PEOPLE CAN SURVIVE THE FALL IF THEIR PARACHUTES FAIL TO OPEN.

A CAMP FIRE, a flash of lightning… it doesn't take much to start a forest fire. Flames quickly move through dried grass and trees, producing thick, suffocating smoke. Temperatures soar to 1,470°F (800°C) or more. Thousands of miles of vegetation, wildlife, homes, and people are at risk. What do you do? CALL THE FIREFIGHTERS!

This firefighter stands behind the flames of a brush burn in Colorado.

FLAMES ARE FOUR TIMES HOTTER THAN A PIZZA OVEN.

THE FIRE TRIANGLE

A fire needs three things to burn: fuel, heat, and oxygen. When a firefighter takes away one of these elements, the fire goes out.

Heat

Fuel

Oxygen

ABOUT 30% OF ALL LAND IS COVERED BY FORESTS. MOST FORESTS ARE IN RUSSIA.

HOW TO FIGHT FOREST FIRES

Firefighters drag long, flexible hoses to the edge of a fire and blast the flames with water. This **cools down** leaves and branches and **cuts off their supply of oxygen.**

Another tactic is to create a fire break by chopping down trees in front of the fire. Firefighters may also start a fire to burn toward the first one. When the fires meet, there is **no more fuel** to burn, so the flames go out.

Sometimes helicopters scoop up giant **buckets of water**, or carry flame retardant to drop on the flames.

FIRE CAN BE USEFUL

When large forest fires burn near roads and houses, they can cause catastrophic damage. However, fires are part of the life cycle of a forest, burning away old dead wood and making way for new plants to grow. So in some areas, small forest fires are started and controlled, as a way of avoiding giant, disastrous blazes later on. These are called **prescribed fires.**

HOW HOT IS HOT?

9,932°F / 5,500°C
Surface temperature of the Sun.

2,500°F / 1,370°C
Steel melts.

1,470°F / 800°C
A forest fire

1,200°F / 649°C
The temperature that a firefighter's clothing can briefly withstand.

572°F / 300°C
Wood catches fire.

230°F / 110°C
Very high sauna temperature, and the most an unclothed person can stand.

212°F / 100°C
Water boils.

98.6°F / 37°C
Human body temperature.

89.6°F / 32°C
Butter melts.

32°F / 0°C
Water freezes.

FIRE EQUIPMENT

A fire engine carries firefighters and water to a fire. On board is a pump that pushes the water through the hoses. Several hoses can be connected to the pump at the same time.

A firefighter's clothing is called "turnout gear." Pants are stored turned down over the boots. In an emergency, the firefighter can jump into the boots and pull up the pants—fast!

Ladders can be more than 100 ft (30 m) long to reach high windows.

Animals escape
During a forest fire, animals try to escape from the heat. They run, or fly away, or burrow under the ground.

This koala was rescued by a firefighter after a forest fire in Australia in 2009. Her feet were injured, so she was taken to a wildlife center to recover.

Fire engines can carry more than 1,000 ft (300 m) of hoses.

BATTLING THE BLAZE

Other common fires include:

Garbage Uncollected garbage and blazing garbage dumps are especially dangerous—firefighters need to know if chemicals are hidden in the pile—some may explode if they come into contact with water.

WHEN THERE IS A FIRE IN A HOUSE, ALERT EVERYONE AND LEAVE THE BUILDING IMMEDIATELY.

Jacket is made from layers of material. The outside is the same flame resistant fabric that race-car drivers wear. The other layers protect the firefighter from heat and water.

Helmet is extremely hard and has a flap of fire resistant cloth at the back to stop burning embers from falling down the back of the firefighter's neck.

Breathing equipment includes an air tank and mask. The firefighter has enough air to last 30 minutes—except when breathing hard.

Tall buildings have fire escape stairs, water sprinklers, and fire extinguishers on each floor. When the fire alarm sounds, everyone has to leave quickly. If anyone is left behind, firefighters may use a telescopic ladder to rescue them.

Cars Most car fires are caused by leaks, electrical or mechanical faults, or worn-out parts.

US AND CANADA 911... UK 999... AUSTRALIA 000... NEW ZEALAND 111...

13

YOU'RE HIGH UP ABOVE A CROWD. In front of you is an open space with a thin wire stretching across it. You have to step out onto the wire, put one foot in front of the other, walk across. And whatever you do, don't look down!

You need lots of practice to be a tightrope walker. A long, flexible pole helps with balance.

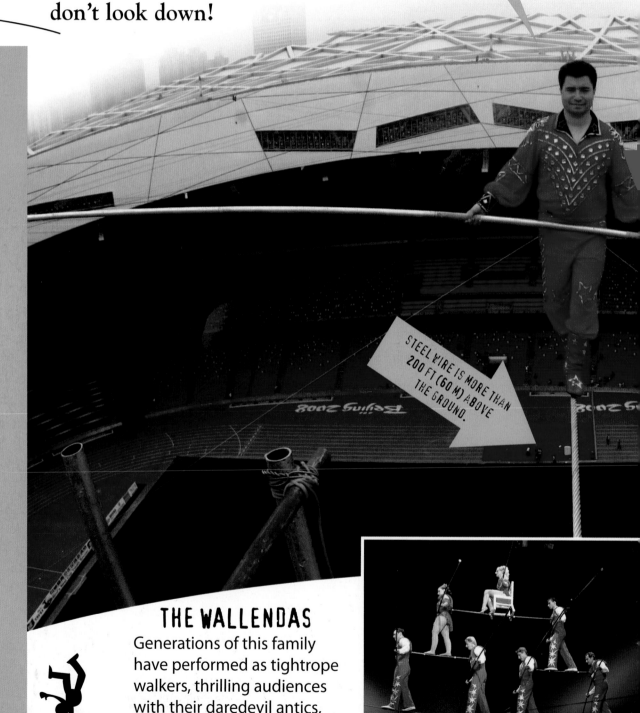

STEEL WIRE IS MORE THAN 200 FT (60 M) ABOVE THE GROUND.

THE WALLENDAS
Generations of this family have performed as tightrope walkers, thrilling audiences with their daredevil antics, often without a safety net.

THE ART OF WALKING ALONG A TIGHTROPE IS CALLED FUNAMBULISM.

dili Wuxor is known in China as **"the prince of the tightrope."** In July 2010, e spent 60 days living and tightrope walking across the Bird's Nest stadium n Beijing, China. He walked around 2½ miles (20 km) a day on a steel wire just 1¼ inch (33 mm) thick.

ird's Nest stadium

circus trick
ghtrope walkers are traditional part of rcus. This performer heading up a slope wire, th one end attached to the ound and the other to the top a pole. It's a 40 degree slope!

... And all performed on a tightrope!

In 2010, stuntman Samat Hasan walked 2,300 ft (700 m) uphill along a tightrope. He was hundreds of yards up in the air—without a safety harness!

In 2007, Johann Traber and Johann Traber Jr. drove a motorcycle 130 ft (40 m) above the ground.

Juggling, handstands, and standing on your head are all in a day's work for a tightrope walker.

THE NARROWER THE SLACKLINE, THE MORE FLEXIBLE IT IS.

GIVE US SOME SLACK!

Slacklining differs from tightrope walking in that you walk on a 1–2-in- (2.5–5-cm-) wide flat nylon webbing, which is stretched between two anchor points. The line is not rigid, but bounces, stretches, and sways... and that's before the high winds are factored in!

DANGER

UP IN THE AIR...

Slacklines are usually made up of a long section of webbing, which may be up to 100 ft (30 m) in length. This is connected to two shorter pieces of webbing— one at each end—which anchor the slackline to a rock or tree.

Freestyle slacklining uses a very slack line. This means it swings wildly!

PEOPLE HAVE SLACKLINED BETWEEN TREES, BUILDINGS, AND ROCKS.

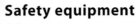

Safety equipment
A harness stops you from falling far if you lose your balance.

When you don't have a safety harness, falling is not an option.

YOU'RE NEVER QUITE IN CONTROL, BUT IT'S THE WOBBLE THAT KEEPS YOU GOING.

Tricklining or lowlining usually takes place on a short line close to the ground. Walkers can practice all kinds of jumps and somersaults.

RECORD BREAKERS

SLACKLINE WALK

A slackliner at Lost Arrow Spire

Name: Scott Balcom
When: July 13, 1985
Where: Lost Arrow Spire, Yosemite National Park

Crossing a slackline to Lost Arrow Spire 3,000 ft (880 m) above the valley floor is not easy! The 55 ft (16.7 m) walk was first achieved by Scott Balcom in 1985.

IT CAN TAKE PLACE 2 FT (60 CM) ABOVE THE GROUND OR 3,000 FT (880 M) UP.

17

Every house, bridge, tunnel, and tower has to be built. That's the job of CONSTRUCTION WORKERS—a hardy breed of skilled workers who do their jobs high above the ground. Dangers include getting caught in saws or drills, electrocution, and falling.

CONSTRUCTION WORKERS SET STEEL BEAMS ON THE 88TH FLOOR OF THE SHANGHAI WORLD FINANCIAL CENTER SUPERSTRUCTURE.

When up high, all workers have to harness themselves to a secure place.

Construction work involves specialized craftspeople working together to get the job done. The job is overseen by engineers, who follow the architect's plans and solve problems as they go along.

Worker using cutting saw

Crane driver

CONSTRUCTION WORKERS ARE CAREFUL TO AVOID HAZARDS...

Jin Mao Tower

Safety first

A construction worker's gear includes a hard hat, bright jacket, gloves, and goggles. Some tools make almost as much sound as a jet engine—so ear protection is a must. Workers also wear a harness that attaches them to high structures.

Helmet

Ear protection

Gloves

Safety goggles

Oriental Pearl Television Tower

TOOLS OF THE TRADE

Modern buildings are built with modern tools. These require skillful handling.

High-speed nail guns eject nails by detonating explosive cartridges. It means a 4 in (10-cm) nail can be fired into solid concrete with speeds as fast as 1,400 ft (427 m) a second!

Jackhammers produce an amazing amount of force to enable them to smash up concrete, but they can also create startlingly loud sounds. Levels of 90 decibels can cause hearing loss if a person is exposed to them for a long time. Workers should wear ear protection.

The sharp edges of chainsaw chains are covered with diamond grit to make them extra sharp. They can slice through concrete, brick, and stone with ease. The chains move at speeds of 1 mile (1.6 km) a minute, so full safety gear is essential—as is paying attention at all times!

Bricklayers, carpenters, electricians, glaziers, pipe-fitters, sheet metal workers, steel and iron workers, heavy equipment operators, concrete finishers, decorators, and more are all needed to build a building.

BURJ KHALIFA

Rising way above the nearby skyscrapers is the enormous shining silver structure of Dubai's giant, Burj Khalifa. This record-breaking skyscraper is the tallest building in the world, and breaks many other records, too, including the building with the most floors.

FACT FILE

THE BURJ KHALIFA UNDER CONSTRUCTION

Height: 2,717 ft (828 m) tall—that's about half a mile (1 km)!

Workers: At peak construction times, 12,000 workers were on site every day.

Support: 194 concrete columns, each 5 ft (1.5 m) wide and 141 ft (43 m) long, are buried 165 ft (50 m) deep in the desert floor.

Speed: There are 57 elevators. They travel at 22 miles (36 km) an hour—that's 33 ft (10 m) per second.

At 206 stories, the Burj Khalifa dwarfs all the buildings surrounding it.

When I'm cleaning windows...

How would you like to be one of the window cleaners? It takes 36 workers 3–4 months to clean all 28,261 glass panels. Their total area is roughly 143,520 sq yd (120,000 sq m) of glass—that's 16½ soccer fields! The Sun's reflection off the glass is so fierce that workers can only work on the building's shaded sides.

NIGHTCLUB ON THE 144TH FLOOR

RESTAURANT ON THE 122ND FLOOR

SWIMMING POOL ON THE 76TH FLOOR

How tall is tall?

The Burj Khalifa building is said to be so tall that you can watch the sunset at the bottom, then go up in the elevator and see it all over again!

LIVING THE HIGH LIFE!

This pool spans three tall towers of the Marina Bay Sands hotel.

THIS SWIMMING POOL IS PERCHED JUST OVER **623 FEET (190 M)** ABOVE THE GROUND.

Singapore is home to the world's highest outdoor swimming pool (of those built in skyscapers, at least!). This is also the longest elevated swimming pool. The pool has a 478-ft (146-m) vanishing edge where the water spills over into a catch basin below.

A high match
A special tennis match between Andre Agassi and Roger Federer was once held on the helipad of the Burj Al Arab hotel in Dubai. The platform is 692 ft (211 m) above ground level.

HIGH PLATFORM!

Name: Grand Canyon Skywalk
What to see: A glass bottom provides a dizzying view.

This amazing horseshoe-shaped walkway curves out just over 70 feet (21 m) from the edge of the Canyon to suspend people ¾ mile (1.2 km) above the Canyon's floor.

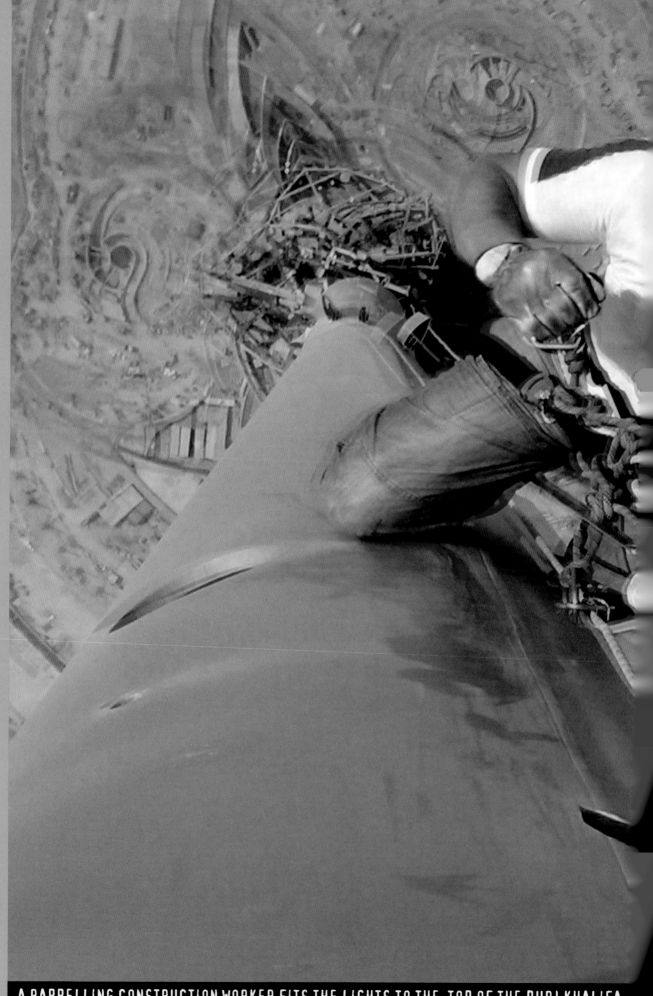

22

A RAPPELLING CONSTRUCTION WORKER FITS THE LIGHTS TO THE TOP OF THE BURJ KHALIFA.

... JUST OVER HALF A MILE (1 KM) ABOVE THE GROUND.

FISHING IN STORMY SEAS

IT'S HEADING TOWARD WINTER and storms rage across the Bering Sea. This might not seem the best time to go fishing, but tough Alaskan fishermen climb into their boats and head out into the waves. Their job—which is among the most dangerous in the world—is to catch crab and they're not going to let the weather stop them.

Freezing conditions

The Bering Sea sits at the top of the world between the Russian Federation and Alaska. Here it is so cold that in the winter part of the sea freezes over. Alaskan fishermen sail close to the ice, since king and tanner crabs prefer to live in freezing waters.

Bering Sea

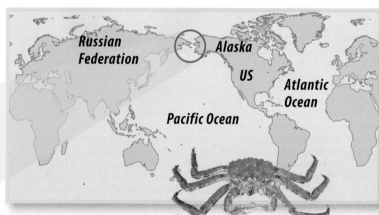

Russian Federation

Alaska

US

Atlantic Ocean

Pacific Ocean

AT BUSY TIMES, FISHERMEN HAVE TO WORK UP TO 20 HOURS A DAY.

Survival suits If a boat is about to sink, a fisherman can climb into his survival suit and zip it up. The suit is watertight and warm enough to keep him alive for hours in freezing waters while he waits to be rescued.

Once a fisherman is in his suit, he floats on his back until help arrives.

Life rafts These are stored in rigid containers. In an emergency, a fisherman throws the opened container into the water. Inside are cylinders of gas that automatically inflate the raft. The crew can then climb down from the sinking boat and clamber into the raft. The cover keeps off wind and rain and is an easy-to-see orange or yellow.

Hauling in crab

To catch crab, fishermen drop huge metal traps, called crab pots, over the side of the boat. They mark each pot with a floating buoy. Crabs crawl into the pots looking for food and get stuck. A couple of days later, the fishermen return and winch the pots back on board. They tip out the crabs and put the adult males, still alive, in a holding tank inside the boat. Females are thrown back into the sea.

Buoys are brightly colored so they are easy to spot.

Crab live on the ocean floor.

An Alaskan fisherman lets off a distress flare in a survival training session.

WHEN A WAR FINISHES, dangerous landmines are often left behind. These will explode and cause horrific injury or death to anyone unlucky enough to step on one. They have to be cleared away. The people who do this are bomb-disposal experts—highly trained workers who risk their lives making the land safe for local people.

If a landmine accidentally explodes, a helmet and visor protect the worker's head, face, eyes, and neck.

Blast-proof body armor protects the shoulders and chest from flying debris.

This mine clearance worker uncovers a landmine in Cambodia.

LANDMINE!

IT IS ESTIMATED THAT THERE ARE ACTIVE MINES IN 70 COUNTRIES AROUND THE WORLD...

LANDMINE!

What is a landmine?

Landmines are explosive devices that sit on, or just under, the ground. They blow up when someone steps on them or drives over them. Other dangerous things left behind after a war include hand grenades or bombs. These are called unexploded ordnance (UXO).

METAL MINE HUNT

Mines are sometimes made of metal and this can be detected when a clearance worker waves a metal detector back and forth across the ground. The metal detector makes a loud whining sound when it is near something metal. Then the worker carefully and gently probes the ground to uncover the mine.

Danger!! Mines!!

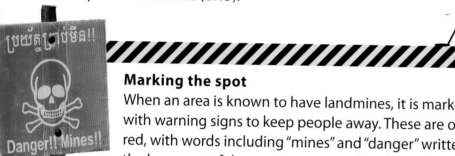

Marking the spot

When an area is known to have landmines, it is marked with warning signs to keep people away. These are often red, with words including "mines" and "danger" written in the language of the country, or a skull and crossbones.

FACT FILE

ANIMAL MINE HUNTERS

Mine clearance experts sometimes use specially trained animals that can sniff out explosives and report back.

During experiments, trainers have tried to teach **honeybees** to find explosives. They put the explosives near sugar-water, which bees like to feed on. The idea is that the bees associate the smell of explosives with the reward of food and swarm over the explosives.

When landmines and other unexploded devices sit in the ground, many leak the smell of explosives into the surrounding soil. Specially trained **sniffer dogs** recognize this smell. They stop, sit down, and look at their handler to show they have found something.

Even in the murky water of a harbor, a trained bottlenose **dolphin** can find a mine. To do this it uses echolocation— it makes clicking sounds, then uses the sound waves that bounce off objects to form a picture of what is there.

The **African giant pouch rat** has an excellent sense of smell. It is trained to link the smell of explosives to food and will sniff out explosives in the field. When it is working, it wears a harness attached to a rope. A handler on each end of the rope helps to guide the rat.

WHEN YOU'RE WALKING UP TO A BOMB, THE ONLY THING YOU THINK ABOUT IS THE BOMB ITSELF.

BECOMING AN EXPERT

Do you want to be a **bomb disposal expert**? Then you'll need to be calm under pressure and have very steady hands. Bomb disposal experts train in the army or while working for bomb disposal organizations. They study the science of explosions and every type of explosive device. And they keep up with new technology so they can work out what might be made into a bomb in the future and how to make it safe.

One way to destroy a landmine or UXO is in a **controlled explosion**. For this, experts attach a small amount of explosives to the landmine. Using a long detonator cord, they move to a safe distance, then press the firing button.

This **Aardvark** is a demining machine that beats the ground in front of it with chains. These blow up any mines in its path. The driver sits in an armor-plated cabin with bullet-proof windows.

Driver's cabin at BACK

Chains at FRONT

34916

SFOR

SFOR E2M

It takes just one hour for the Aardvark to clear an area the size of about seven tennis courts.

BOMB DISPOSAL ROBOTS CARRY CAMERAS SO VIDEO FOOTAGE OF THE BOMBS...

When this unexploded bomb was found in Dorset, England, 4,000 people had to evacuate their homes while it was made safe.

OLD BOMBS

Occasionally unexploded bombs from World War II are discovered. They were left behind when the war ended more than 60 years ago. They may still be dangerous, so bomb disposal experts are called in to make them safe.

BOMB DISPOSAL ROBOTS

Bomb disposal robots can disarm a bomb or carry it to a place where it can be blown up safely. Since they are operated from a distance, people are protected from any explosion.

The **Dragon Runner** robot is small enough to be carried on a person's back. It travels over rough ground on tracks, like a tank, and has a long arm that can dig around a suspicious object and carry it away.

... CAN BE SENT BACK TO THE OPERATORS WHILE THEY STAY OUT OF HARM'S WAY.

29

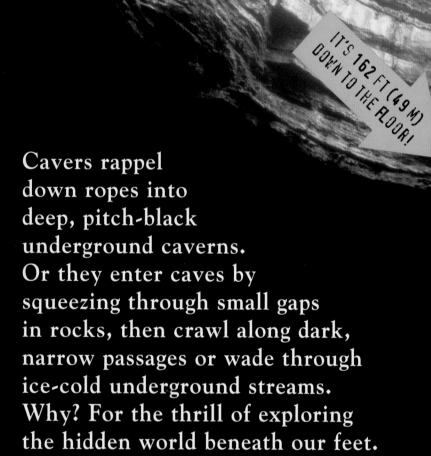

IT'S 162 FT (49 M) DOWN TO THE FLOOR!

Cavers rappel
down ropes into
deep, pitch-black
underground caverns.
Or they enter caves by
squeezing through small gaps
in rocks, then crawl along dark,
narrow passages or wade through
ice-cold underground streams.
Why? For the thrill of exploring
the hidden world beneath our feet.

CAVING STEP BY STEP

A caver puts on layers of
warm clothing, boots with
nonslip treads, and a hard
hat with a light at the front.
He picks up his ropes and
squeezes into the cave.

Watch your step
Caves are full of dark,
narrow crevices to
explore. Water flows
underfoot, making the
rock very slippery.

FOR SAFETY, CAVERS GO EXPLORING WITH OTHER PEOPLE...

Going down—cavers explore Neversink Pit in Alabama.

Camp campsite
On long treks, cavers camp overnight in a cave. Even on short trips cavers should carry water, food, and first-aid kits. This caver is filling up his water bottles with water dripping from the cave ceiling.

DANGER BELOW

It's hard to rescue someone who's stuck in a cave deep underground. So cavers take care not to get lost in tunnels, fall into deep pits, or get hurt by rock falls. And that's not all...

IS THE FLOOR SOLID?

Rocky caves can be wet and slippery to walk in, but it's even worse to walk on a floor that's not there! When a stream

flows over a cave floor, it leaves behind sediment. A mineral layer called **flowstone** may form on top. It looks like a solid floor but really it's just a thin crust, like ice on a frozen pond.

This caver climbs barefoot, and very carefully, over flowstone.

GETTING BREATHLESS

Some caves have bad air. Bat droppings, decomposing plants, volcanic activity, and even the rocks themselves can all release deadly gases that make cavers feel **dizzy** or become **unconscious**. Some cavers use matches to test for the gas carbon dioxide. A small or no flame spells danger and the caver knows to turn back—quickly!

WHAT'S THE WEATHER?

When you're underground, it doesn't matter what the weather outside is doing, right? Wrong! Cavers must be aware of heavy rain. A **sudden downpour** can flood underground passages quickly, trapping anyone below.

.. AND ALWAYS TELL SOMEONE WHERE THEY ARE GOING AND THE TIME THEY EXPECT TO RETURN.

31

Name: Nuno Gomes
Record: World's deepest cave dive
(and world's deepest sea dive)

Nuno Gomes was born in Portugal, but moved to South Africa at age 14. There he discovered cave diving, and in 1996 he broke the record for the deepest cave dive—927 ft (282.6 m) down into Bushmansgat sinkhole. It was so deep, the water pressure crushed two of his flashlights. Nuno also won the record for the deepest sea dive. In June 2005, he reached a depth of 1,044 ft (318.25 m) in the Red Sea.

DIVERS EXPLORE A VAST NETWORK OF CAVES AND TUNNELS IN MEXICO.

THE LOST DIVER

It was 1991 and a diver was exploring flooded caves in the mountains of Venezuela. Swimming through long, dark tunnels stirred up mud in the water, making it hard to see. Soon he lost contact with his dive buddy— and he couldn't find his way out!

The diver's friends called expert cave divers Steve Gerrard and John Orlowski to search for him. They flew all the way from Florida, and when they reached the cave, the diver had been missing for 36 hours. They didn't hold out much hope of finding him alive. But they began their search. It was hard to see in the murky water, but they kept looking. Eventually they swam into an underground cave and surfaced in an air pocket... and they were not alone! The diver was there, too, and he was ALIVE! So they led him out to safety.

For experts only!
Cave diving is more risky than either caving or diving alone—there's no escape if you run out of air trapped [in] a dark maze of flooded caves. Cave divers unravel a rope as they swim, so they can follow it back to the entrance. And they keep a constant check on their air supply to make sure they have enough left to get back safely.

STUDYING CAVES IS CALLED SPELEOLOGY. SPELEOLOGISTS EXPLORE CAVES TO DISCOVER

Waterproof diving flashlight

AMAZING CAVES

For a sense of achievement, there's nothing like exploring the most extreme caves the world has to offer. Like these, for example...

LONGEST...
Mammoth Cave in Kentucky is the longest known cave system in the world—more than 390 miles (630 km) of passageway have been explored so far. It would take about 130 hours to walk this distance! At first glance, there seems to be no life in the passageways, but it's thought that 200 animal species live in them, from bats to eyeless fish, which have evolved to live in the dark.

DEEPEST...
It's a long way down to the **Krubera Cave** in the country of Georgia—7,188 ft (2,191 m). The deepest cave in the world has cold, muddy, narrow passages, and steep drops. Krubera is also known as the Voronja Cave, which means "Crows' Cave" in Russian, because crows nest in the cave entrance.

... AND VERY HOT
Cavers visiting the **Cueva de los Cristales** ("Cave of Crystals") in Mexico must wear suits filled with ice! The cave is full of very humid warm air. If this is breathed in, it may condense (turn to water) in the caver's lungs, which can be fatal. To prevent this, cavers use breathing equipment that provides cool, dry air.

THE CAVE OF CRYSTALS IN MEXICO WAS DISCOVERED WHEN MINERS ACCIDENTALLY

BROKE INTO THE CAVE. SOME OF THE CRYSTALS ARE MORE THAN 33 FT (10 M) LONG.

SOME SNAKES inject a deadly poison, called venom, when they bite. This could kill you, but it doesn't have to. You can be given a medicine called antivenom and make a full recovery. Antivenoms are made using the actual snake's venom itself. And it's a SNAKE HANDLER'S JOB to extract it.

Venom drips out of the fangs of a diamond rattlesnake. Untreated bites from this snake can be fatal.

Collecting venom

Snakes store venom inside their heads, just behind their eyes. To extract it, a snake handler first stretches a piece of rubber across a glass cup. Then he picks up the snake and holds it on both sides of its head. The snake bites through the rubber, releasing venom through its hollow fangs into the cup.

Preparing antivenom

While still in the cup, the venom is freeze-dried, which turns it into crystals. Trained technicians (wearing protective masks to avoid breathing in venom), scrape the crystals from the cup. This is then sent to a laboratory for processing.

Small doses of the processed venom are injected into big draft horses. This doesn't hurt the horses. Instead, their bodies build up antibodies that protect them. Then some of their blood is extracted in the same way that a human blood donor gives blood. The antibodies are taken from this blood and purified into an antivenom that can be used on humans.

COLLECTING VENOM FROM A SNAKE IS CALLED "MILKING."

FIRST, CATCH YOUR SNAKE

Some antivenom laboratories breed their own snakes. Other snakes are caught in the wild. To catch a snake, an expert handler uses a long stick with a hook on the end. He waves the stick over the snake's head. While the snake is distracted, the handler quickly picks up its tail in one hand. He hooks up the head and bundles the snake into a bag.

What happens when you are bitten by a snake?

Even venomous snakes don't inject venom every time they bite. However, if they do, several things could happen, depending on the type of snake. Common symptoms of snake bites are:

headache
vomiting
double vision
stomach pain
paralysis (you can't move)

I don't feel so well!

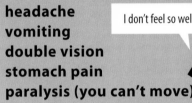
A rattlesnake made this painful bite.

Snakes are released back into the wild after they have been milked three times.

SSSSSSO... YOU WANT THE FACTS ON VENOM?

- Venom is a form of saliva.
- It takes hundreds of milkings to make a single dose of antivenom.
- Antibodies in the antivenom attack venom and neutralize its effects.
- Some kinds of snake venom fetch more than $85,000 an ounce.

Sedge viper

DEADLY SNAKES

Here's a handful of the world's most venomous snakes.

Tiger rattlesnake *US*
This snake has heat-sensing pits on its face so it can sense warm-blooded prey, even in the dark. It has a rattle on the end of its tail to warn you that it's there.

Hook-nosed sea snake
Indian and Pacific Oceans
This snake has a flattened tail for swimming and nostrils that close when it's under water. Although it is extremely venomous, it is unlikely to bite unless it feels threatened.

Russell's viper
India, Sri Lanka, Pakistan
The Russell's viper lives in grassy areas and in rice fields. Farmers are often bitten by this snake while planting and harvesting their crops.

Inland taipan *Australia*
This is the most venomous land snake, but it is not aggressive. It feeds mostly on rodents, such as rats. It bites its victim, then waits for it to die, to avoid getting hurt itself.

Boomslang *Southern Africa*
The boomslang grows to more than 6 ft (2 m) long. It lives in trees and is camouflaged by its greenish-brown skin. It strikes without warning.

Black mamba *South Africa*
You'll find black mambas living in pairs or small groups. This nervous snake will slither away when a human is near. However, if threatened, it lifts and shakes its head. Then it will dart in, bite, and slither away.

SO YOU WANT TO WORK WITH ANIMALS?
Here are ideas for things you might NOT want to try.

The performer can hold this position for several seconds.

CROCODILE WRESTLER

Not many people would try to show a crocodile who's boss, but some people do it for a living. Croc wrestlers swing them by the tail, lift them up, and even put their heads in the animal's mouth. The trick is to wave a stick around the croc's head and send it into a trance, so it keeps its mouth open.

SHOWTIME!

Performers entertain zoo visitors by wrestling with crocodiles in Pattaya, Thailand.

BUCKING BULL

RODEO RIDER

In a rodeo show, riders compete against each other by riding horses bareback, calf roping, and bull riding. They mount the horse or bull in a small gated pen. The gate opens and the animal bucks and snorts its way into the arena. The rider holds a rope with one hand, but rarely stays on for long. When he falls, he risks breaking bones, or being trampled or gouged by the bull.

The rider has to stay on the bull for eight seconds.

THE DOG CATCHER QUICKLY TIGHTENS THE NOOSE SO THE DOG CAN'T BITE HIM.

AN ANGRY BULL WILL ATTACK ITS RIDER, SO RODEO CLOWNS DISTRACT IT WHILE THE RIDER ESCAPES

BIG GAME VET

When a wild animal gets sick on a game reserve, it's the job of the local vet to help it get better. When that animal is as dangerous as a lion, the vet needs to be very brave! The vet has to fire a tranquilizer dart into the animal before she can even think of taking a closer look.

This lion is ready for medical treatment.

A lion pounces, grabs its prey with its sharp claws, and bites...

SO, WHAT ARE YOU GOING TO DO ABOUT THIS TOOTHACHE?

DOG CATCHER

The dog catcher's job is to find stray dogs and put them into kennels until an owner is found for them. Most dogs are perfectly friendly, but some are bred for fighting or may have been badly treated, and require careful handling. Dog catchers use a long pole with a noose of cable at one end, which they slip around the dog's head. They can then hold the dog at a distance without getting bitten.

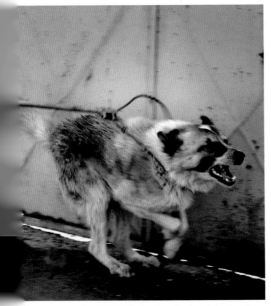

A stray being caught by a professional dog catcher.

NOT ALL ANIMALS ARE FRIENDLY

The most deadly animal of all is the **mosquito**. Mosquitoes carry the malaria parasite, which they inject into humans when they bite. Malaria causes fever, sickness, and eventually death. Yet, every year hundreds of people volunteer to be bitten and become sick in the interests of medical science. Ouch!

Collecting wild honey can be a tricky and dangerous job. Not only do you face being stung by **bees**, but often you also have to climb sheer rock faces or tall trees to get at the combs. In places such as Cameroon, Cambodia, and Nepal, men set out to harvest the honey armed only with a smoking branch or the juice of a local shrub rubbed into their skin to keep the bees at bay. Although bee stings are painful, it would take at least 500 stings before they would prove fatal.

We've all seen those amazing nature programs on television, but it takes real courage and dedication to get footage of some animals. Wildlife cameramen and researchers have to trek through inhospitable places or spend hours under water, patiently waiting for that perfect shot. And you never know when that **dangerous animal** you've been looking for might creep up behind you...

Want to find out how **sharks** behave in the wild? Well, the only way to get up close and personal is to get in the water with them. Just make sure you're in a safety cage when you watch them!

THE CROCODILE HAS THE MOST POWERFUL BITE OF ANY LIVING ANIMAL.

PLENTY OF DRIVERS STAY HOME WHEN THERE'S SNOW outside. But driving along frozen roads is just part of the job when you're a truck driver in cold climates. On the northern routes of Alaska, Scandinavia, Siberia, and Canada, truck drivers brave blinding snow and biting cold to deliver food and fuel to remote communities. Or they carry vital drills or pumps to mines or gas fields. It's an icy drive—but someone has to do it!

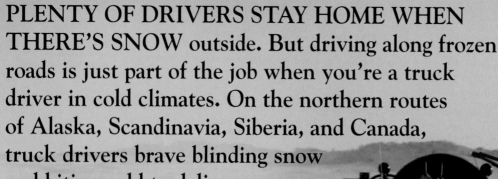

Siberian winter road
Trucks deliver huge pipes to the snowy Siberian gas fields.

DEEP TREADS ON THE HUGE TIRES PROVIDE GRIP ON PACKED SNOW AND ICE, TO PREVENT SKIDDING.

BUILDING AN ICE ROAD, CANADIAN STYLE

Each year, crews build roads over frozen lakes in northern Canada. These roads can be more than 300 miles (500 km) long and reach out to isolated villages and diamond mines.

Clearing a path
Snow plows clear away snow to help speed up the freezing and thickening of the snow.

Measuring the ice
There are weight limits along the ice road. To set these limits, crews measure the thickness of the ice using ground-penetrating radar or a drill called an ice auger. This is the same kind of auger that scientists use to dig holes in Antarctica when they study the ice sheet there.

ROAD SAFETY

When you are driving on ice roads, there are a few things you might want to know about...

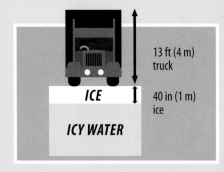

13 ft (4 m) truck

ICE

40 in (1 m) ice

ICY WATER

Fully loaded supertankers are superheavy, weighing up to 35 tons. To travel safely, they need at least 40 in (1 m) of solid ice under their wheels.

If trucks don't keep to a **constant, slow speed,** the wheels can create waves in the water under the ice. These waves move ahead of the vehicle and can cause ice near the shoreline to break.

MAXIMUM 50

Thickening the ice

Road crews pump water from the lake over the surface, where it freezes in layers. Or they spray water into the air, causing ice crystals to fall on the road, speeding up how quickly the ice forms. Sometimes a mesh is laid over the surface and frozen into place.

When a truck drives over the ice, tiny cracks can be created, making a sound like breaking glass.

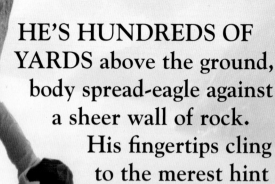

CLIMBING UP ROCK FACES

CLIMBING REQUIRES NERVES OF STEEL AND A COOL HEAD. FROM HERE, YOU'VE ONLY GOT TWO CHOICES—UP OR DOWN.

HE'S HUNDREDS OF YARDS above the ground, body spread-eagle against a sheer wall of rock. His fingertips cling to the merest hint of a hand hold—the rock climber remains totally focused on the wall in front of him. One wrong move—and it's a long way down.

RAPPELLING

Once he reaches the top, the climber has to get back down. One way to do this is to rappel—lower himself on a rope that's anchored to the rock. The rope passes through a belay device, which acts as a break to stop the climber from coming down too quickly.

Climbing alone, without a harness, ropes, anchors—or climbing partner—is the ultimate climbing experience. Falling is not an option, since the climber has nothing to stop her from crashing to the ground. All she has are a pair of close-fitting shoes, a bag of chalk, and her skill, strength, and judgment.

Bouldering involves climbing up or sideways across boulders. It focuses on problem-solving and technique rather than endurance needed over long climbs. Sometimes boulder climbers put crash mats underneath them, just in case they fall.

CLIMBING HAZARDS

Falling To stop themselves from falling, climbers rope themselves to anchors in the rock, or climb in pairs so only one person is actively climbing at one time.

Rock falls Even small pieces of falling rock can result in injury. So climbers often choose to wear helmets.

Heat stroke There's little shelter on a rock face—climbers wear sunblock and carry water so they don't burn or dehydrate.

Bad weather Climbers need to watch the weather—in rainstorms dry canyons become rivers, trapping climbers on cliff faces.

Painful arms The muscles in a climber's arms are often working very hard and this can cause buildup of a chemical called lactic acid. This hurts, so climbers can often be seen shaking their arms to remove the buildup.

Scaling a skyscraper
Some climbers have taken climbing to new heights. Alain Robert, a French climber, is known as "Spiderman" because of his love of climbing skyscrapers. However, a lifetime of bouldering and clinging to narrow ledges has left him with permanently bent fingers. He also developed a fear of heights after a number of high-rise falls.

It's all in a day's work
for some people. Wind turbine technicians, electricity linesmen, telephone engineers, construction workers, and tree surgeons often need to learn climbing and rappelling skills to help them reach high tree branches, telephone cables, and turbine motors.

EQUIPMENT
Don't go climbing without the right equipment—and make sure you know how to use it!

Ropes These are essential in most rock climbing. There are lots of different kinds including:
Dynamic ropes, which are designed to stretch. The more they stretch, the less the climber is jarred if he falls. But a stretchy rope also means the climber will fall farther, so there is more chance he'll hit overhanging rock.
Semi-static ropes are less stretchy and are used for rappelling.
Dry ropes are waterproofed, so they don't freeze solid in cold weather. They are used in mountaineering.

Belay device When a climber threads rope through a belay device, it acts a bit like a brake and holds on to the rope if the climber falls.

Spring-loaded cams, nuts, runners, and slings are all devices that are placed in the rock or wedged into crevices to guide a climber's rope and take his weight if he falls.

Hand chalk Climbers often carry a bag of chalk dust with them. They rub it into their hands to absorb sweat and help them grip the rock.

ROCK FALLS CAN HAPPEN UNEXPECTEDLY AND KNOCK A CLIMBER OFF BALANCE.

ENTER THE DANGER ZON

Climbing is a hazardous hobby
Rocks may crumble above a
climber. Loose slabs of snow
present a constant threat of
avalanches. Sudden weather
changes are common on
mountains—thick fog or violer
snow storms can make even th
most hardened climber turn ba

Climbers may need ropes and collapsible ladders to cross wide crevasses in glaciers.

Walking on ice
As a mountaineer climbs, he may
find his path blocked by large, gaping
cracks in the ice. These are crevasses
and they can be up to 65 ft (20 m)
wide and 150 ft (45 m) deep.

Camping out
Some climbs take several days
(they are known as big wall
climbs), and climbers may have
to sleep overnight on the rock
face. Imagine setting up a
temporary camp on a narrow
ledge and sleeping inside a mini
tent (a bivouac bag). If there is
no ledge, a climber may have
to hang a "camp-bed" called a
portaledge on the rock face
and sleep on that.

High up in a mountain
temperatures will drop well below
-15ºF (-26ºC), so mountaineers wear
layers of windproof, waterproof clothing
to help them keep warm. At high altitudes
the amount of oxygen also drops, which
can lead to an illness called mountain
sickness—a climber may feel dizzy or
tired or be sick and will have to return
to a lower altitude to recover.

A PERSONAL CHALLENGE

Mountaineers are always setting
themselves challenges—for
example, planning to climb all
peaks over 13,000 ft (4,000 m)
in the Alps. One of the ultimate
challenges is the Seven Summit

THE WORLD'S HIGHEST MOUNTAIN, EVEREST, WAS FIRST CLIMBED IN 1953...

AN ICY CLIMB

It's not easy climbing a wall of ice. It's super slippery, while climbing routes keep changing as the ice melts and refreezes, leaving no permanent anchor points for a climber's ropes. This climber is using two ice axes. She swings them alternately to stick them into the ice before pushing herself up with her legs.

Metal spikes, called crampons, help the climber grip the ice.

TO THE RESCUE

Mountaineer Claude Ratte was climbing down a mountain ridge in Denali National Park, Alaska. Then he fell, crashing and tumbling down a steep slope, before coming to a stop 2,000 ft (600 m) from where he started. He'd hurt his face, leg, and ankle—but he was alive! His satellite phone was still working, so he called 911 to get help. Then he waited.

It took park rangers about three hours to reach the injured man. They strapped him onto a stretcher, then hauled him back up to the ridge. Then they lowered him down the other side to the rangers' camp and a waiting rescue helicopter that whisked him away to recover in the hospital.

The Seven Summits are the highest peaks on each continent. They are:

NORTH AMERICA Denali (Mount McKinley) in Alaska: 20,320 ft (6,194 m)

AFRICA Kilimanjaro in Tanzania: 19,340 ft (5,892 m)

SOUTH AMERICA Aconcagua in Argentina: 22,841 ft (6,962 m)

ANTARCTICA Vinson Massif: 16,050 ft (4,892 m)

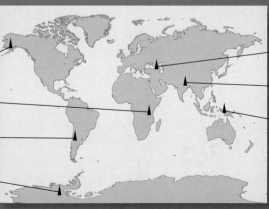

EUROPE Elbrus in Russia: 18,510 ft (5,642 m)

ASIA Everest: 29,029 ft (8,848 m)

OCEANIA Carstensz Pyramid (Puncak Jaya) in New Guinea, Indonesia, on the Australian continental shelf: 16,024 ft (4,884 m)

CLIMBING A ROCK FACE

TOMMY CALDWELL NEARS THE TOP OF THE GRAND OL' OPRY IN COLORADO.

TOMMY IS A WORLD-CLASS CLIMBER, DESPITE HAVING LOST PART OF A FINGER.

47

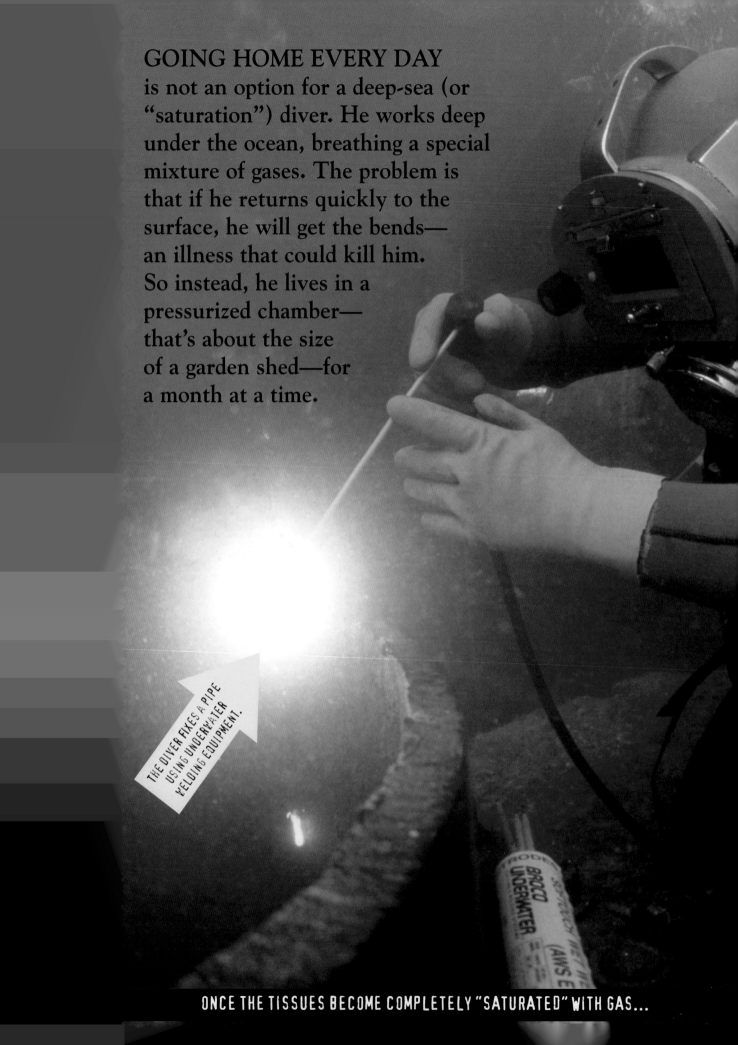

GOING HOME EVERY DAY

is not an option for a deep-sea (or "saturation") diver. He works deep under the ocean, breathing a special mixture of gases. The problem is that if he returns quickly to the surface, he will get the bends— an illness that could kill him. So instead, he lives in a pressurized chamber— that's about the size of a garden shed—for a month at a time.

THE DIVER FIXES A PIPE USING UNDERWATER WELDING EQUIPMENT.

ONCE THE TISSUES BECOME COMPLETELY "SATURATED" WITH GAS...

Home away from home

When they are not out diving, saturation divers stay in a pressurized living chamber. This means they only have to adjust to normal pressure once—when the job is completed—since the chamber's pressure is kept the same as the water they work in. The chamber sits on the support ship and divers return to it after each shift, traveling up in the diving bell.

This living chamber is on board a ship in the Barents Sea.

The amount of time a diver spends in decompression depends on how deep he goes and how long he stays at that depth. After he has been at depth for several hours, the length of decompression stays the same— about 50 ft (15 m) a day.

A SATURATION DIVER WORKS MORE THAN 300 FT (90 M) BELOW THE SURFACE.

THE BENDS
The bends, or decompression illness, happens when a diver returns to the surface too quickly.

DANGER

A diver breathes a mixture of gases including helium and oxygen. As he goes deeper, the weight of the water forces the gas in his blood into the surrounding tissues until they become saturated (full).

If he comes up too quickly, the gas dissolves out again and forms bubbles, like when you undo the top on a bottle of soda. It causes extreme pain. The trick is to come up slowly so that bubbles do not form. This is called decompression, and it can take days.

The diving bell

A diving bell acts like an elevator between the seafloor and the living chamber on the surface and hangs on a cable. It is small and cramped, allowing transportation between the living chamber and the work area for just two or three divers at a time.

... A DIVER CAN WORK SAFELY AT DEPTH FOR DAYS AT A TIME.

HOW DEEP DO THEY DIVE?

◎ **scuba diver breathing air**— 130 ft (40 m)

◎ **surface-supplied diver**— 160 ft (50 m)

330 FT (100 M)

660 FT (200 M)

1,000 FT (300 M)

1,300 FT (400 M)

1,600 FT (500 M)
◎ **saturation diver**—1,600 ft (500 m)

2,000 FT (600 M)

2,300 FT (700 M)
◎ **hard-suit diving** (divers wear a bulky suit that has the same pressure inside as on the surface)— 2,300 ft (700 m)

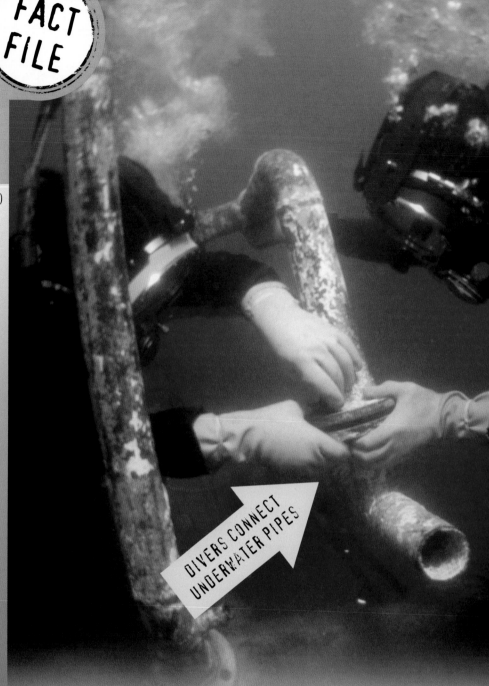

DIVERS CONNECT UNDERWATER PIPES

WHAT'S THE JOB?

Most divers work in the oil industry, installing, checking, and repairing drilling rigs and pipelines. Or they salvage ships and aircraft that have sunk, or submarines that get stuck on the ocean floor. Other divers work in shipyards, repairing the outsides of large ships, or are involved in building bridges and dams. There are even diver medics who can give first aid underwater and emergency treatment to divers who get the bends.

LIVING CHAMBERS AND DECOMPRESSION CHAMBERS HAVE ROUNDED WALLS...

HOME COMFORTS

A living chamber houses six to eight men and has bunks, a shower, and a toilet. Anything they need—food, medicines, clean clothes, hot drinks—has to be delivered through a series of airtight valves and doors. The important thing is to keep the pressure inside the chamber at a controlled level, so only the outer door opens directly to the atmosphere.

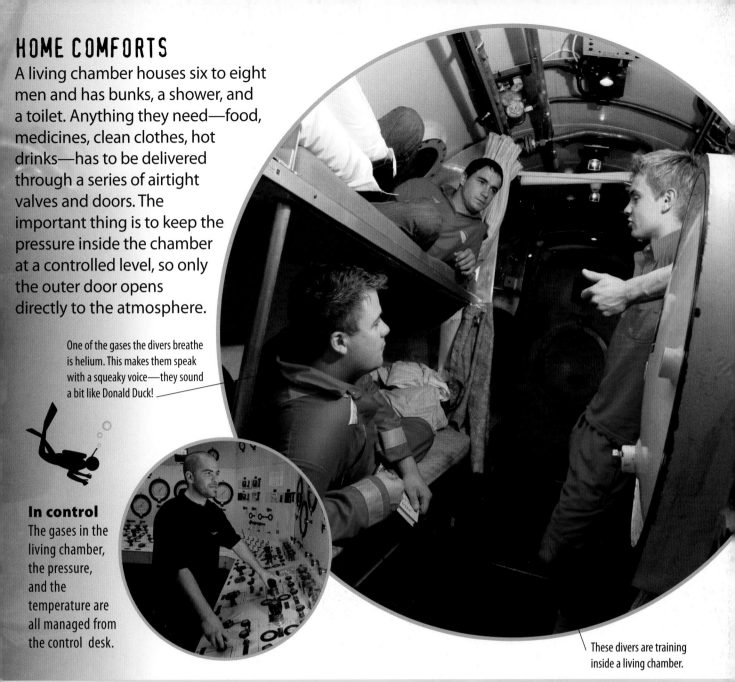

One of the gases the divers breathe is helium. This makes them speak with a squeaky voice—they sound a bit like Donald Duck!

In control
The gases in the living chamber, the pressure, and the temperature are all managed from the control desk.

These divers are training inside a living chamber.

SURFACE-SUPPLIED DIVING

For dives down to around 160 ft (50 m), divers are connected to the surface by an umbilical. This supplies them with breathing gas, plus communication with the control desk. Divers carry breathing bottles in case the umbilical fails.

When he arrives back at the surface, the diver goes straight into a decompression chamber, where the gases in his body will be slowly returned to their normal levels.

A diver heads down into the water.

Decompression chambers on board a ship.

... SINCE THIS IS THE STRONGEST SHAPE FOR COPING WITH THE PRESSURE.

A HELICOPTER DROPS YOU OFF at the top of an extremely steep, snowy mountain. There is only one way to go, and that's down—very fast. The skier pushes off and heads downhill, doing her best to avoid crashing into rocks or trees, or falling into crevasses, or off the edge of the mountain itself.

EXTREME SKIERS CAN REACH SPEEDS OF UP TO 50 MPH (80 KM/H)

EXTREME SKIING SLOPES RANGE FROM 45° UP TO 70°

Heliskiing sees an adventurous skier taken into hard-to-reach areas by helicopter. Then he's off on fresh powder snow for a wild ride down.

EXTREME, OR BIG MOUNTAIN, SKIING REQUIRES A LOT OF SKIING EXPERIENCE...

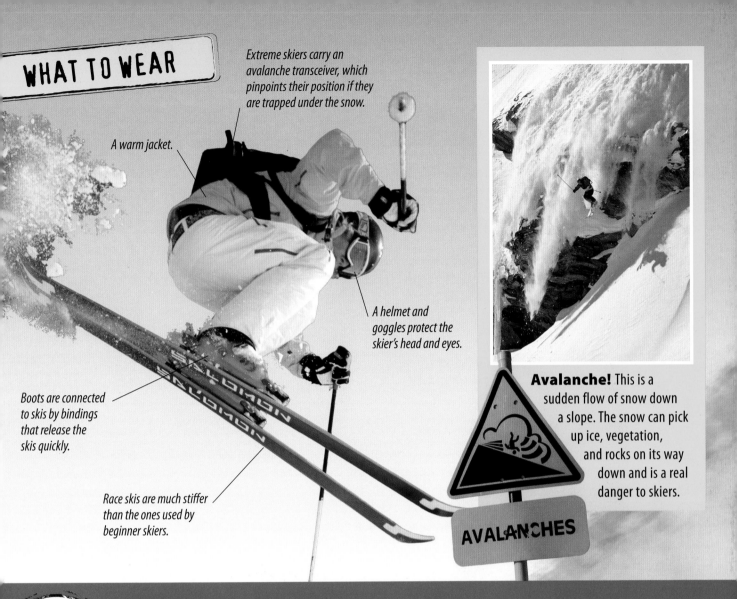

WHAT TO WEAR

Extreme skiers carry an avalanche transceiver, which pinpoints their position if they are trapped under the snow.

A warm jacket.

A helmet and goggles protect the skier's head and eyes.

Boots are connected to skis by bindings that release the skis quickly.

Race skis are much stiffer than the ones used by beginner skiers.

Avalanche! This is a sudden flow of snow down a slope. The snow can pick up ice, vegetation, and rocks on its way down and is a real danger to skiers.

AVALANCHES

FACT FILE

OTHER TYPES OF SKIING

A skier somersaults, showing the skill of freestyle skiing. In this sport, skiers perform aerial jumps, spins, and twists after jumping off a ramp. Freestyle aerial skiing was made an Olympic sport in 1994.

Snow kiting is when the skier is attached to a kite, which pulls him along—even uphill or into the air.

Dogs or horses take on the work of pulling in skijoring, in which people compete to be the fastest on skis. Sometimes the dogs wear special boots to protect them from cold snow and ice.

... AND EVEN THEN IT IS A LEAP INTO THE UNKNOWN. IT IS AN INCREDIBLY DANGEROUS SPORT.

BURIED UNDER THE GROUND are valuable fuels and precious metals, such as gold and platinum. To get them out, mine companies dig deep shafts and tunnels. This is where miners go to work, using powerful drills to dig into the rock. Trucks and elevators take the precious metals back to the surface.

Protective helmet with lamp attached.

Miners drill holes then pack them with explosives.

SOME MINERS WORK IN TUNNELS JUST 3 FT (90 CM) HIGH

These South African miners are digging for one of the most expensive metals in the world—platinum. They work in low, narrow tunnels called stopes. To stop the roof from falling in, they prop it up with metal pillars.

THINGS THAT ARE MINED: GOLD, SILVER, COPPER, COAL, NICKEL, OIL, GAS, DIAMONDS...

HOW DEEP IS A MINE?

Mines can be as high as the tops of mountains and as deep as 2½ miles (4 km) under the ground.

Height of Appalachian Mountains: 3,000 ft (915 m)

Original land surface

Ground level

Dangers down a mine

Working down a mine is dark, dirty work. In addition to the bone-jarring drilling into rock, there is the danger of poisonous gases, clogging dust, searing temperatures, explosion, fire, and rock falls. Main tunnels are tall and wide, but closer to the rock face miners may only be able to travel on their hands and knees.

A miner drills in a cramped South African gold mine.

Deep heat

The deeper you go into the ground, the hotter it gets. On average, the temperature increases by 5 degrees Fahrenheit for every 300 ft (100 m) of depth. However, sometimes shallow mines are much hotter than deep mines because they are close to areas of volcanic activity.

Bursting rocks

Mining companies spend millions trying to keep their mines cool enough to work in. Rocks are heated by the scorching temperatures of Earth's core and are under tremendous pressure from the weight of the rock above them. When tunnels are built through these rocks they can shatter or explode without warning. This is what miners call "rock burst."

Average temperature of Earth's surface 59°F (15°C)

Gold elevator

Miner's elevator

Sometimes the tops of mountains are lopped off to get to coal just under the surface. That's what's happened in the Appalachian Mountains. Some of these mountains used to be more than 3,000 ft (915 m) high before they were strip-mined for their coal.

Shaft mines are the deepest kind of mine. They have vertical shafts that go straight down into the ground, and elevators to carry miners up and down. Among the world's deepest mines are the gold mines of South Africa. One of these is almost 2½ miles (4 km) deep.

2½ miles

2½ MILES DEEP

The temperature at the bottom of the deepest gold mine reaches 136°F (58°C).

... RUBIES, SAPPHIRES, EMERALDS, IRON, ZINC, AND TIN.

A GOLD MINER'S DAY AT WORK

1 **It can take more than an hour to reach the rockface** from the top of the pit. First, the miner climbs into a cagelike elevator. He's lowered deep below the surface. Once he reaches the right level, he walks or travels in a train to his place of work.

About 40 miners travel in the elevator together.

3 **Miners use pneumatic drills** to make holes in the walls of the tunnel. They put explosives in the holes—then stand back. The explosion loosens tons of rock and rubble. The miners scrape out the gold-bearing rock and pour it into a collection shaft called a box hole.

2 **Miners work in teams** in low, narrow tunnels called stopes. They follow the seams that contain the gold, which twist and turn through the rock.

Metal pillars hold up the roof.

A miner drills into the rock face.

4 **The gold-bearing rock falls into open train trucks.** These are pulled to the exit shaft and hauled up to the surface.

A train hauls gold-bearing rock to the exit.

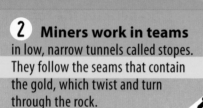

TRAPPED—33 CHILEAN MINERS

In August 2010, 33 gold miners were working underground. Then the roof caved in. They were trapped!

Rescue workers drilled narrow boreholes into the mine to search for the men. Then, 17 days after the accident, the rescue workers pulled out the drill and found a note attached to it. It said "We're okay in the shelter, all 33." The miners were alive!

A huge rescue mission began. Rescuers drilled a shaft, only just as wide as a man. Then each miner in turn squashed into the one-man elevator and was winched up to the surface. All 33 miners were rescued.

Miner Jimmy Sanchez is brought to the surface after more than two months underground.

HEIGHT = ABOUT 24 FEET (7.3 M)

WHY MINE GOLD? GOLD NEVER RUSTS OR TARNISHES,

MONSTER DRILL

This roadheader drills into rock and soil to make tunnels in a mine. Star-shaped wheels at the front push the soil under the roadheader and onto a conveyor belt for removal.

It's 40 ft (12 m) long!

SIZE MATTERS

Miners move millions of tons of soil and rock before they get anywhere near the gold or coal they want to dig out. This unwanted material is called waste, or overburden. Enormous machines dig it out, load it onto trucks, and carry it to processing plants or dumping sites near the mine.

GIANT TRUCKS

This truck is too big to drive on an ordinary road.

Big movers
Mining companies use the largest dump trucks in the world. Fully loaded, these weigh up to 600 tons (545 metric tons) and travel at 40 mph (64 km/h).

Giant trucks at the Batu Hijau copper and gold mine in Indonesia. This open-pit mine is 1 mile (1.6 km) wide.

ASTRONAUTS SPACEWALK

ASTRONAUTS WORK OUTSIDE THE INTERNATIONAL SPACE STATION (ISS).

THEY ARE ONLY ATTACHED BY THIN WIRES—210 MILES (340 KM) ABOVE NEW ZEALAND.

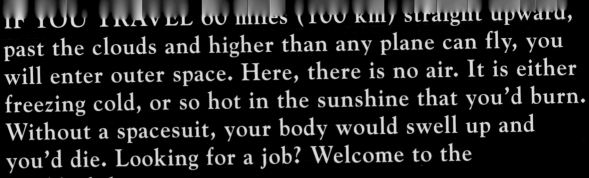

IF YOU TRAVEL 60 miles (100 km) straight upward, past the clouds and higher than any plane can fly, you will enter outer space. Here, there is no air. It is either freezing cold, or so hot in the sunshine that you'd burn. Without a spacesuit, your body would swell up and you'd die. Looking for a job? Welcome to the world of the astronaut.

Space nothingness

For a place full of billions of stars and galaxies, space is surprisingly empty. Between the stars, there is almost no air, dust, or other matter. Scream as loud as you like, you will not make a sound because there is nothing to carry the noise from your mouth. No one will hear you.

So what's the job?

Astronauts travel and work in space. The jobs they do vary—the pilot flies the spacecraft, but the mission specialists and flight engineers make sure the spacecraft is working properly and perform repairs. They also conduct scientific work such as studying Earth, carrying out experiments on plants, and making new substances in space.

The training

It takes about two years for successful candidates to train to be astronauts.

They learn how to survive landing in an ocean, as well as hot jungles and cold mountains, in case they accidentally come down there at the end of a mission.

Training involves practicing space walks under water, because the movements feel similar to being in space.

ALONE IN SPACE? NOT REALLY...

WHAT IS OUT THERE?

Astronaut needed

The first astronauts were young, military fighter pilots. Now the job is open to more people. The space agencies that hire and train astronauts usually choose people who meet tough standards. There is a lot of competition. To stand a chance of being chosen you usually need to:

- *be between 5 ft 2 in (157.5 cm) and 6 ft 3 in (190.5 cm) tall*
- *be healthy and fit*
- *have good eyesight*
- *hold a college degree in math, science, or engineering*
- *have worked in the above areas, or have an advanced degree, or be a teacher, or a jet aircraft pilot*
- *get along well with people—there's not much room in a spacecraft and you'll be up there for a while.*

Getting used to weightlessness requires several trips in an aircraft called the "Vomit Comet."

Pilots practice flying in a model that's just like a real spacecraft.

Outer space

This contains the planets and stars. There is practically no air between them, just a few scattered dust particles and hydrogen atoms.

The edge of space

Most experts agree that outer space starts 60 miles (100 km) above sea level.

The atmosphere

We live inside the Earth's atmosphere. It contains the air that we breathe. The air gradually gets thinner the farther up we go.

Mount Everest

Everest is the tallest mountain on Earth. It is in the Himalayas mountain range and reaches 29,029 ft (8,848 m) above sea level. That's roughly 5½ miles (9 km). Mountaineers need oxygen tanks to help them breathe at that height.

Highest homes

Many people live in the Andes Mountains in South America and the Himalayas Mountains in Asia about 3 miles (5 km) above sea level. Lowland people would find it difficult to breathe the thin air at this altitude.

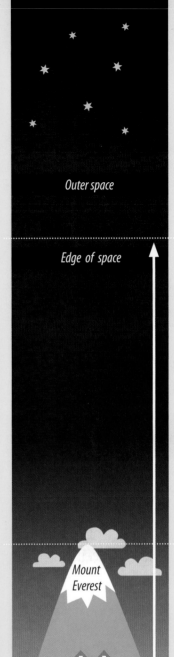

Outer space

Edge of space

Earth's atmosphere

Mount Everest

Highest homes

Sea level *We measure the height of land against the average height of the ocean.*

I did it! I'm an **ASTRONAUT** now.

Floating around

In space, astronauts and anything else not tied down, are weightless. During training, astronauts experience short bursts of weightlessness in a specially adapted plane. It roller coasters up and down in the sky, and at the top of each "hill" and as it races back down, astronauts feel weightless.

Going up...

Going down...

SPACE STATION

If you are an astronaut, you might live in space for six months at a time. Your home is the International Space Station (ISS). This is a kind of laboratory, where up to six astronauts live and work for months on end.

The first part of the space station was sent into orbit in 1998, and since then other modules have been added and are used for living quarters, life-support systems, and laboratories.

The ISS orbits Earth about 16 times a day. If you LOOK UP at dawn or dusk, YOU CAN SEE IT with your naked eye. It looks like a slow-moving star crossing the sky.

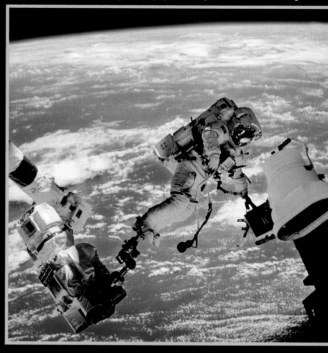

Making repairs or installing new equipment requires hours of training.

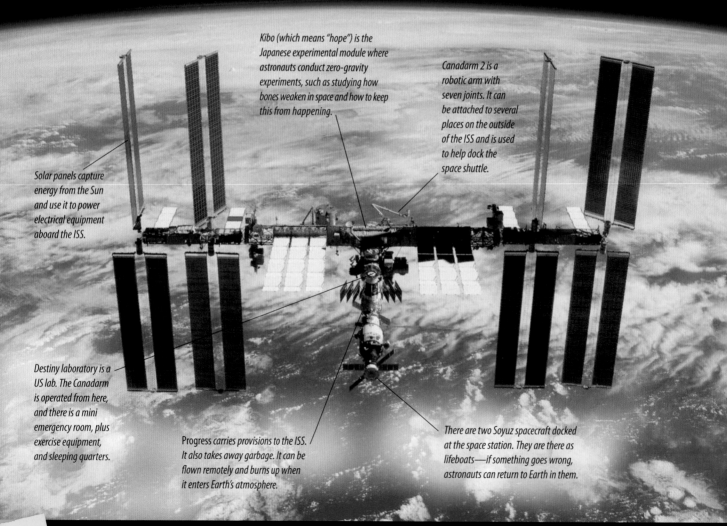

Kibo (which means "hope") is the Japanese experimental module where astronauts conduct zero-gravity experiments, such as studying how bones weaken in space and how to keep this from happening.

Canadarm 2 is a robotic arm with seven joints. It can be attached to several places on the outside of the ISS and is used to help dock the space shuttle.

Solar panels capture energy from the Sun and use it to power electrical equipment aboard the ISS.

Destiny laboratory is a US lab. The Canadarm is operated from here, and there is a mini emergency room, plus exercise equipment, and sleeping quarters.

Progress carries provisions to the ISS. It also takes away garbage. It can be flown remotely and burns up when it enters Earth's atmosphere.

There are two Soyuz spacecraft docked at the space station. They are there as lifeboats—if something goes wrong, astronauts can return to Earth in them.

THE ISS IS THE SIZE OF A FOOTBALL FIELD...

ASTRONAUT'S OUTFIT

Inside the protective world of a spacecraft, an astronaut wears ordinary, comfortable coveralls. But outside is another matter. When she's sent out to repair the spacecraft or conduct experiments, she needs something that will keep her alive. So she wears a spacesuit—a kind of mini survival outfit.

Lights

Visor is like a two-way mirror. It reflects the heat and glare of the Sun, and although you can't see the astronaut's face, she can still see out.

Astronaut carries oxygen tanks on her back so that she can breathe.

Jet propulsion unit helps astronaut steer.

Red stripes help identify individual astronauts.

Suit is puffed up because it is full of air.

Color wise

Spacesuits are usually white, to reflect the heat of the Sun. However, astronauts traveling in a space shuttle wear orange suits for takeoff and landing. Then if something goes wrong and they have to parachute to safety, they will be easy to spot.

The space shuttle cannot be launched if it is raining, very windy, or too cold. On one occasion, the launch of space shuttle Discovery was delayed when woodpeckers pecked holes in the insulation around the fuel tank.

A "hole" lot of trouble!

The biggest danger to a spacecraft is being hit by space junk, such as an old satellite. Something as small as a fleck of paint, traveling at high orbital speeds, could make a hole in a spacecraft. Anything larger than a football is monitored from the ground, so spacecraft can move out of its way.

IT'S A RECORD!

Space exploration has given us many "space firsts," including:

July 1946 The first animals sent to the edge of space were fruit flies aboard a US V-2 rocket.

November 3, 1957 The first animal sent into orbit was Laika, a stray dog from the Soviet Union, on board *Sputnik 2*. Laika died during the trip.

April 12, 1961 The first man to go into space was Soviet Union cosmonaut Yuri Gagarin, in the spacecraft *Vostok*. He orbited once around the Earth and parachuted to safety from the spacecraft just before it landed.

July 20, 1969 The first man to step onto the surface of the Moon was astronaut Neil Armstrong. When he stepped down from the *Eagle* landing craft he said, "That's one small step for man, one giant leap for mankind."

April 19, 1971 The first space station, Soviet Union's *Salyut 1*, was launched. Its three-man crew died on the return trip to Earth.

April 12, 1981 The first reusable spacecraft, the space shuttle *Columbia*, was launched from the Kennedy Space Center in Florida. After more than 20 successful flights, it broke up on reentry into Earth's atmosphere in 2003, killing all seven crew.

April 30, 2001 The first person to pay for a flight into space boarded the ISS. He was Dennis Tito, a 60-year-old American millionaire. He stayed for a week, at a cost of more than $20 million.

... IT ORBITS EARTH AT AN ASTONISHINGLY FAST SPEED— 5 MILES (8 KM) PER SECOND.

63

The most spectacular type of surfing, BIG-WAVE SURFING is when people ride waves that are more than 20 ft (6 m) high. The upside is an incredible adrenaline rush. The downside is that a breaking wave can push a surfer 50 ft (15 m) under the water. He has less than 20 seconds to get back to the surface—before another wave hits...

EXTREME SURFERS HAVE BEEN KNOWN TO RIDE WAVES AS HIGH AS 70 FT (21 M). THAT'S ABOUT AS TALL AS A SEVEN STORY BUILDING.

SURFING BIG WAVES

Surf's up
Surfboards are long and light and shaped so surfers can steer them through waves. They are made of foam or fiberglass, which helps them float. Surfers spread wax on the top of their boards, then rough it up with a comb. This helps them grip with wet feet.

The experienced surfer's board of choice is the gun. It is long and good for paddling into large waves. Both ends are pointed. The gun can be more than 12 ft (3.7 m) long.

Short, wide boards are called fishes or eggs. They start at just under 5 ft (1.5 m) long and are fast and easy to turn.

Shortboards are generally between 5–7 ft (1.5–2.1 m) long and are good for twisting and cutting through the water. They are the most popular type of board.

Longboards, or Malibus, are usually 9 ft (2.7 m) or longer and have a round nose. They are the most stable type of board and the best kind for a beginner.

TO TRAIN, SURFERS PRACTICE HOLDING THEIR BREATH IN CASE THEY ARE HELD UNDER

Helicopter helper

When a surfer rides a big wave, a camera crew may film him from a hovering helicopter. Occasionally a surfer rides a wave at night, using the helicopter lights to see the way.

Hitching a lift

When waves are a long way out, a surfer can be towed by a jet ski. The driver is the surfer's lifeline—after surfing, he picks him up and takes him back to shore. Drivers and surfers take turns driving and surfing.

THIS SURFER SPEEDS ALONG AT AROUND 30 MPH (48 KPH), AS HE RIDES A 40 FT (12 M) WAVE CALLED JAWS.

The strength and speed of the wind makes the water start to ripple and then become choppy.

As the waves get closer to shore their energy and the decrease in water depth pushes the water upward, making the waves bigger.

When waves combine, larger rounded swells begin to travel in the same direction as the wind.

The back of the wave moves faster than the front. The wave becomes too high and breaks onto the shore.

What makes a wave BIG?

Waves are made by strong winds blowing over a giant expanse of water, such as an ocean. What's under the water also makes a difference. As the water reaches the shore, the lower part of the wave crashes into the seabed and slows down. The top of the wave carries on until it falls over onto the shore.

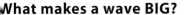

THE WATER. THEY TRY NOT TO PANIC—IT BURNS UP TOO MUCH OXYGEN.

DANGER ZONE

Big-wave surfing is only for super-brave, super-skilled surfers. Here's why.

Strong currents called rip tides can pull surfers out to sea. If you're unlucky enough to get caught up in a rip, you might just be able to swim across it—not against it—and reach the other side before you are swept away.

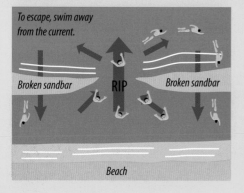

To escape, swim away from the current.

Broken sandbar RIP Broken sandbar

Beach

Shark! Shark! is a cry surfers never want to hear. Sharks don't often attack, but when they do, a surfer can lose a limb or even his life.

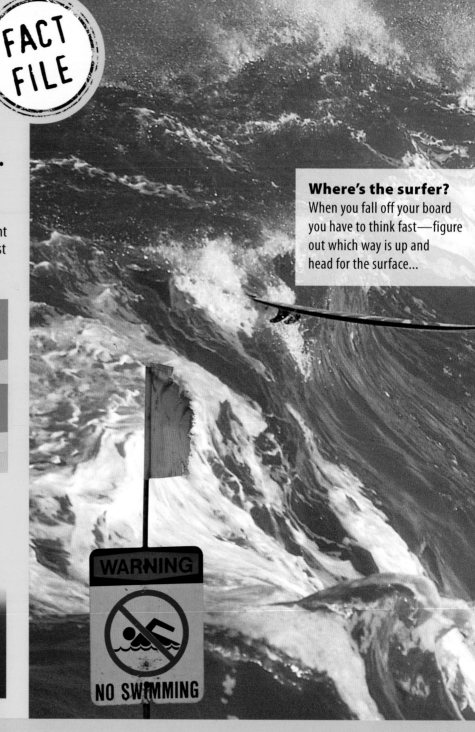

Where's the surfer?
When you fall off your board you have to think fast—figure out which way is up and head for the surface...

WARNING
NO SWIMMING

WIPEOUT
When a surfer is held under water by a wave, it's called a wipeout. If he can't get back to the surface quickly, he may even drown. The best way to survive is to take a deep breath before you go under, curl up and protect your head.

Like on a road, surfers try to stay out of the way of moving traffic. This surfer is trying to escape from his own jet ski. The driver has jumped off.

These huge waves only occur during the winter months when ocean swells and strong winds combine.

RECORD BREAKER

Name: Mike Parsons
Record: Riding a wave of more than 70 ft (21 m) at Cortes Bank, California, in 2008.

If you want to surf the really big waves you've got to be in shape. Mike Parsons, one of the world's top big-wave surfers goes to the gym, swims, and mountain bikes, as well as spending hours surfing.

WARNING

STRONG CURRENT

YOU COULD BE SWEPT AWAY FROM SHORE AND COULD DROWN IF IN DOUBT, DON'T GO OUT

Sandbanks, reefs, and rocky seabeds can all inflict nasty cuts and bruises and even knock you unconscious if you hit them. Surfers need to find out what's lurking beneath the surface before they ride that wave.

Watch the board— it may come back and hit you. Many surfing injuries are caused by surfboards ramming into surfers. It may not be your own board— many accidents are caused by other surfers.

SOMEONE FALLS over a cliff, or a boat sinks, leaving a man stranded in the water. He manages to keep afloat while he calls for help. Minutes later he hears a roaring sound and looks up. Hovering overhead is a helicopter—and a rescuer is being winched down to help.

A HELICOPTER CAN FLY AT MORE THAN 125 MPH (200 KM/H).

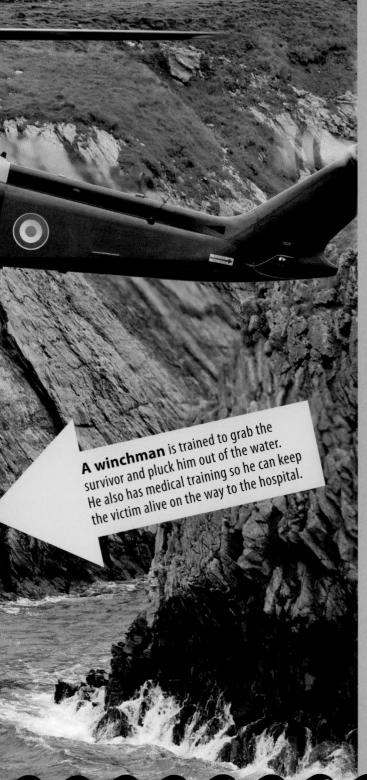

THE PILOT HOLDS
A STEADY POSITION
DESPITE BUFFETING WINDS.

A **winchman** is trained to grab the survivor and pluck him out of the water. He also has medical training so he can keep the victim alive on the way to the hospital.

SIGNS OF DISTRESS

When a sailor needs help, he can light a flare to signal that he is in trouble and show rescuers where he is. Flares are like fireworks, and just as dangerous. Many sailors carry a thick glove with their flares, so they can light them without burning their hands.

Red and orange flares signal a life and death problem. White flares let other boats know you are there so they don't run into you. Flares can be handheld or fired into the air like a rocket.

Hand-held flares

CALLING FOR HELP

Most seagoing vessels carry a marine Very High Frequency (VHF) radio. This transmits and receives messages, but not at the same time. In an emergency, use channel 16—it's the international distress channel and is monitored by rescue services.

You can either talk OR listen on a VHF radio. When you have finished talking, let the other person know that it is their turn by saying "OVER."

When calling for help, repeat your words three times. You can start by saying "MAYDAY," which is understood around the world to mean "HELP." A distress call might go like this:

MAYDAY! MAYDAY! MAYDAY!
This is the *Ocean Rose*! *Ocean Rose*! *Ocean Rose*! We are sinking! Request immediate assistance! OVER!

B-7115

中國海監

AN "H" IN A CROSS TELLS A PILOT THIS IS A HOSPITAL HELIPAD.

A helicopter lands on the roof of the Ruijin Hospital in Shanghai, China.

PILOT IN CONTROL

The search and rescue pilot is in the air within 30 minutes of receiving a call for help. He knows the approximate location of the victim and heads off in the right direction. Once he is airborne, the control center gives him more precise details of what the mission may involve.

A Swiss air rescue helicopter races to the scene of an accident. Time is critical when people have been hurt.

To the rescue
Rescue helicopters are equipped with satellite navigation systems, search radars, and several radios. They can also pick up signals from emergency transmitters that some boats carry on board. These signals travel to a satellite in space before they reach the pilot.

TRAINED HELICOPTER PILOTS HAVE TO DO AT LEAST 100 HOURS OF SPECIALIZED TRAINING...

MORE HELICOPTER RESCUES

At the ready

A helipad needs to be ready for action all day, every day. It has lights around the edge so the pilot can see where to land when it's dark. And under the surface is often a heated coil to melt snow and ice, so helicopters can land in winter. The name of the hospital is written on the roof alongside the "H," so pilots know where they are and where to touch down.

HOSPITAL LANDING

The last thing a critically injured person needs is to get stuck in traffic, but a helicopter can take her directly to hospital. The pilot radios ahead to alert hospital staff and gives an outline of the patient's injuries.

The patient is wheeled into the hospital building. An elevator carries her down to the trauma unit where doctors and nurses are waiting.

Seeing in the dark

Some search and rescue helicopters are equipped with an infrared sensor. This detects heat given off by a person and helps find him when it is cloudy or dark. Rescuers can also wear night vision goggles. These boost the available light so it is easier to spot someone who needs help.

Looking through night vision goggles

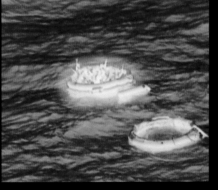

This life raft is invisible in the dark—that's until rescuers look for it using night vision goggles.

Rescue on ski slopes in the French Alps.

Mountain rescue

Even a rescue helicopter cannot land on a steep mountainside. It hovers over a fallen skier or climber while rescue workers strap him to a rigid stretcher.

In 2000, a family is rescued from flood waters in Mozambique.

Flood rescue

When rivers burst their banks, roads become flooded, leaving people stranded. Helicopters can carry them to emergency shelters on higher ground.

This climber's foot was broken by falling rocks in Yosemite National Park.

Cliff top rescue

Large national parks, such as Yosemite in California, have their own search and rescue services. In Yosemite, this helps around 150 people each year.

WITH A BACKWARD STEP, A BUNGEE JUMPER FALLS A HAIR-RAISING 160 FT (49 M)

N THE FAST LANE—that's
these thrill seekers want
s they fly, fall, swim,
drive through the
pages. Are they
lled, super-
or just
zy?

THE PILOT HANGS HORIZONTALLY UNDER THE WINGS.

Hang gliding

A hang glider is a kind of aircraft. It has a kitelike wing and a metal frame with a harness attached—but no wheels or engine. To fly it, the pilot straps himself into the harness, lifts the hang glider above his head, then runs down a slope... and right off the edge of a cliff! The idea is that the wing catches the air and he will soar and glide safely to the ground below.

A wing walking display team performs in Gloucestershire, England.

WING WALKING
For wing walking, this is what you do.

Climb on top of a small plane, strap yourself into a stand, and wait for the plane to judder into life. The plane races along the runway, then lifts off. You're up and away—on the top of a plane! Your face starts to flap around in the force of the wind. You try to smile, but don't have full control of your facial muscles. Still, you're having fun!

A WING WALKER PERFORMS STUNTS AT SPEEDS OF MORE THAN 100 MPH (160 KM/H).

Formation flying

They make it look easy. But flying nine fast jet aircraft close together, at speeds of over 400 mph (640 km/h), is something only the very best pilots can achieve. During displays they come as close as 100 ft (30 m) to the ground. Alongside their superior flying skills, what keeps them alive is practice, practice, and more practice.

The Red Arrows—the UK's Royal Air Force Aerobatic Team.

PLANES ARE JUST 6 FT (1.8 M) APART WHEN THEY PASS EACH OTHER.

Colored trails are made from vaporized diesel fuel mixed with dye.

I'VE CHANGED MY MIIIIIIND! (Too late.)

Bungee jumping off Victoria Falls Bridge, Africa.

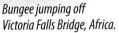

BUNGEE

BUNGEE JUMPING

This scary sport involves jumping from a great height with only a long elastic cord to save you. The cord is tied around the jumper's ankles, and the other end is attached to a high structure, such as a crane or bridge. She jumps off the crane... and the cord stretches, enough to make her feel she will crash headfirst into the ground— but not so much that she actually does!

DIVING WITH SHARKS

Not every kind of shark attacks humans. That's a comforting thought when you are out in the ocean in a wetsuit and mask, watching sharks swim all around you. Great white sharks are dangerous, as are tiger sharks. Nevertheless, there are people who swim with sharks just for fun. Fear is part of the attraction, and getting out in one piece is part of the reward.

Eek!

These Caribbean reef sharks eat fish and large crabs (not people).

STORM CHASING

Most people run for cover at the first sign of rain. Not storm chasers. They study weather maps and satellite images looking for the most extreme kinds of weather—thunderstorms, hailstorms, tornados. Then they drive out to meet them.

DANGER

Extreme weather can bring hailstones the size of tennis balls. These dent cars, smash windshields, and can easily kill. If a storm chaser goes out in a hailstorm, let's hope he's wearing a crash helmet!

A tornado in South Dakota.

BULL RUNNING

It's 8 o'clock in the morning and the streets of Pamplona, Spain, are quiet and tense. Someone fires a rocket. This is the signal that the gate to the Santo Domingo corral is open—and a herd of wild bulls is charging into the town. Men start to run. It's about ½ mile (848 m) to the bullring and the bulls quickly catch up. The men must jump out of the way to keep from being trampled.

Wheee! It feels like I left my stomach at the top, but there's only a couple more seconds of freefall until I hit the water.

THE KAYAKER LEANS FORWARD—BUT NOT TOO FAR OR HE MIGHT FALL OUT.

KAYAKING OVER A WATERFALL

How's this for a test of strength as well as nerves? Extreme kayakers paddle a small, one-man boat (called a kayak) down a raging river. They are heading toward a waterfall, but they don't stop—they go over with it!

RECORD BREAKER

Name: Pedro Olivia
Date: March 2009
Record: 127 ft (38.7 m) waterfall drop

This is Brazilian Pedro Olivia, who hit speeds of 70 mph (113 km/h) in March 2009 when he dropped 127 ft (38.7 m) over the Salto Belo Falls in Brazil. He plunged headfirst into the waters below—and lived to tell the tale.

ONLY MONTHS LATER, PEDRO'S RECORD WAS BROKEN BY TYLER BRADT'S 187 FT (57 M) DROP.

WALL OF DEATH

In this motorcycle stunt bikers drive around the vertical walls of a steep pit. If they drive too high, they fly out of the top. If they slow down, they tumble to the bottom.

A wall of death in New Delhi, India.

PARKOUR IS ABOUT ADAPTING YOUR MOVES SO YOU CAN TRAVEL OVER OBSTACLE

PARKOUR

This is a way of traveling across the buildings and rooftops of cities without using any equipment—just the human body, and whatever climbing places, handholds, and landing spots the buildings themselves have to offer. Runners jump across gaps many stories above the ground, where any misjudgment or slip may lead to injury or even death.

Parkour originated in France, and is a way of climbing, jumping, rolling, and swinging from one place to another. **Freerunning is similar** to parkour, except it is more about creative moves, such as showy somersaults.

One of the first things to learn is how to jump and land—when you land, you roll and keep moving forward on to the next move.

WE HOPE YOU HAVE ENJOYED EXPERIENCING LIFE ON THE EDGE...

Monster truck stunts

If you like big machines, you'll love what happens at a monster truck rally: souped-up, oversized trucks performing wheelies and jumping over cars. The driver is usually fairly safe, since he's strapped into his seat. Spectators have to stay out of the way.

During a show, trucks often crush cars under their giant wheels.

IN YOUR PATH.

EXTREME IRONING

Something that started as a joke is now (almost) a sport. It's called extreme ironing, and it's a way to make chores more exciting. All you need is an ironing board, an iron, and a place where ironing doesn't normally take place. You carry your equipment there, iron a shirt or two, and have your picture taken.

RECORD BREAKER

On a freezing day In January 2009, a team of **86 British divers** claimed the record for the most people ironing underwater—or at least pretending to—at the same time. (The ironing was not a success and their clothes stayed wet and crinkled!)

See you later! I'm just leaping onto the ledge and you're leaving already!

When you can't go rock climbing because you have ironing to do—just take it with you!

animal mine hunters 27
antivenom 36, 37
astronaut 58, 59, 60, 61, 62, 63
avalanche 44, 53

bends 48, 49
Bering Sea 24
big-game vet 39
big-wave surfing 64, 65, 66, 67
bomb-disposal expert 26, 28
bomb-disposal robot 29
bull running 76
bungee jumping 72, 75
Burj Khalifa 20, 22

Canadian ice road 40, 41
cave diving 32
caver 30, 31, 33
climbing 46
construction worker 18, 19, 20, 21, 22
controlled explosion 28
crevasse 44
crocodile wrestler 38
Cave of crystals 33, 34, 35

diving bell 49
dog catcher 39

emergency numbers 12, 13
extreme ironing 79

firefighter 10, 11, 12, 13
fisherman 24, 25
flares, emergency 25, 69
formation flying 75

hang gliding 74
helicopter rescue 68, 69, 70, 71
helipad 21, 70, 71

ice climb 45
International Space Station (ISS)
  58, 59, 62

kayaking 77
  Krubera cave 33
  landmine 26, 27

  Mammoth cave 33
  mine clearance 26, 27, 28, 29
  mining 54, 55, 56, 57
  monster truck stunts 79
Mount Everest 45, 61

night vision goggles 71

parkour 78
prescribed fire 11

rappelling 22, 30, 42
  rock burst 55
  rock climbing 42, 43, 44,
    45, 46, 47
  rodeo rider 38
  rope walking 14, 15

saturation diving 48, 49, 50, 51
seven summits 44, 45
sharks, swimming with 76
Siberian winter road 40
skiing 52, 53
skydiving 4, 5, 6, 7, 8, 9
slacklining 16, 17
snake handler 36, 37
storm chasing 76
surface-supplied diving 51
survival suit 25

trucking 40, 41
turnout gear 12

unexploded ordnance (UXO) 27, 28

venom 36, 37
Very High Frequency (VHF) radio 69

wall of death 78
wing walking 74

ACKNOWLEDGMENTS
The publisher would like to thank the following for their kind permission to reproduce their photographs:
(Key: a-above; b-below/bottom; c-center; f-far; l-left; r-right; t-top)
Action Plus: 78-79b; **Alamy Images:** Greenshoots Communications 51tr, 51cl, 51bc, 54, 56tc, 56-57b, Corbis Flirt 40bl, 40-41, 44bc, 45tl, David Fleetham 51br, Jim Goldstein 60-61, 64bl, Craig Ingram 43crb, Mark A Johnson 74t, 74b, 75t, 75br, 79t, Mark A. Johnson 65cra (inset), Matthew Jones 21bl, 21br, 24br (inset), 24-25, 26, Steve Bloom Images 31bl, 32bl, 37clb, 38tl, 38-39b, 39tc, 39cl, Mark Tipple / The Underwater Project 66bl, David Wall 4bl, 4bc, 5br, WaterFrame 69tr, Jim West 11cl, 11bl; **Barcroft Media Ltd:** 77b; **Bryan & Cherry Alexander / ArcticPhoto:** Arctic Images 24cl (inset); **Corbis:** John Abbott / Visuals Unlimited 31cr, Craig Tuttle 60bl, 60br, 61clb, 61crb, 61bl, 61br, 63t, 64-65, 66clb, 66crb (inset), 66br, 66-67 (main picture), 67clb (inset), 67crb (inset), 67bl, 67br, 71clb, Yves Forestier 15bc, 18bc, 18-19, 18-19b, 19tr, 19br, Thorsten Henn / Nordicphotos 3br, Kamal Kishore / Reuters 70b, 71tr, 71c, 71bc, 71br, 75cl, 76bl, 78t, Frans Lanting 53t, 53tr (inset), 55cl, 55bc, 56cla, 56clb, 56bl, 57br, Don Mason 42bc, 42-43t, 43tr, 43c (inset), 43cr, 43bc, 43br, Paul A Souders 30-31, 32-33, 36bl, 37tr, 38tr, 38bl, Vince Streano 13t, US Coast Guard 21c, 25tr, 25br, 27cl, 27cr, 27bl, 28tr; **Dorling Kindersley:** Charles Van Dugteren 64fbr, Howard Kuflik www.kuflik.com 69br, Richard Leeny / Courtesy of the Aberdeen Fire Department, Maryland 12c, Harry Taylor 55clb (rock), 55fbl (rock); **Dreamstime.com:** Alix 19tc, Ivan Paunovic 5cr, Yykkaa 20; **Fotolia:** Flying_Wizard 6bl; **Getty Images:** AFP 20tr, 27tr, 27bc, 27br, 29bl, Barcroft Media via Getty Images 4br, 4-5, 5bl, 6tr, 6-7, 7tr, 7br, Ron Chapple 63b, 64bc, 64br, Chad Ehlers 75bl, National Geographic 30tc, 31tr, 33cr, 34-35, Martin Harvey 33tr, 33br, 37b, John Kelly 42-43b, 49tl, Colin Meagher 2bc, 3bl, 71cr, 76t, 77 (main picture), Carsten Peter 76cr, Dave Saunders 52bl (inset), 56cra, Tyler Stableford 2br, 5bc, 10-11, 12tr, 13br, 14br, 14-15, 15cr, 15br, 16br, 16-17t, 17tc, 17cl, 17bl, 17br, Gordon Wiltsie 41cr, 41br, 44t (main picture), 44cl (inset), 44cr (inset); **Courtesy of Nuno Gomes:** 32; **Chris Hunter:** 28tl; **Imagestate:** Shari L Morris / AGE Fotostock 11tr; **Masterfile:** R Ian Lloyd 6tl, 7cr; **Ministry of Defence Picture Library:** © UK MOD Crown Copyright 2011, 29br, UK MOD Crown Copyright 2011 2bl, 68-69; **MRP Photography:** 57t; **NASA:** 60cb, 62 (main picture); **North News and Pictures:** 22-23; **Photolibrary:** Philippe Giraud 12tl, 12br, 20tl, 36, National Geographic Society 3bc, OM3 OM3 53br, James Reeve 41bl; **Press Association Images:** Barry Bachelor 29tr, Chen Huanlian / ColorChinaPhoto / AP 70-71; **Reuters:** China Daily 15tr, Vivek Prakash 21t, Stringer Australia 12bl; **Rex Features:** 79br; **Science Photo Library:** Richard Folwell 40br, 48-49, 49br, Peter Menzel 27tl, NASA 50, 55tl, 55tl, 55bl (cosm explosion), 58-59, 62tr (inset), Duncan Shaw 13bl; **Specialist Stock / Still Picture** P Royer / Blickwinkel 53cra (inset); **SuperStock:** Flirt 72-73, imagebroker.net 53bl, 53bc, Painted Sky Images 1br, 17tr, 46-47, StockTrek 28-29, 30br, 31br, SuperStock 8-9; **Wikimedia Commons:** Mough 28bl; **Will Wissman:** 52
Jacket images: Front: **Getty Images:** Joe McBride; Back: **Corbis:** China Daily / Reute All other images © Dorling Kindersley For further information see: www.dkimages.com

WITH SPECIAL THANKS TO...

... British Parachute Association • Longmont Fire Department • Alaska Department of Fish and Game • Mines Advisory Group (MAG) • National Speleological Society • National Cave and Karst Research Institute • Australian Reptile Park • Northwest Territories Department of Transportation • British Mountaineering Council (BMC) • Interdive Services Ltd • Camborne School of Mines / University of Exeter • Peter Bond • Shaun McGrath • Maritime and Coastguard Agency (MCA)